ISBN: 0-8010-7727-3

Scripture verses are from the Revised Standard Version, ©
1946, 1952 by Division of Christian Education of the Na-
tional Council of the Churches of Christ in the United States
of America.

Printed in the United States of America

Unto Us a Child

O come, let us worship and bow down, let us kneel before the Lord, our Maker!   (Ps. 95:6).

I fold my daughter, my first-born, in my arms. She is so warm, so fragile, and yet surprisingly strong. See how she kicks! I confess that until this moment my uppermost thoughts have been for my wife. It was not an easy pregnancy. It was not an easy birth.

But now these anxieties melt away in the supreme joy of holding this "bone of my bones, and flesh of my flesh." My wife looks at us both with eyes of love and contentment. We are now a circle. We are no longer a couple, one to one, but a family.

O Lord, I thank you for the loan of this new life, for a little while ours to nurture and teach and cherish. What an awesome responsibility it is. Be with us day by day. Show us how to help her grow into the kind of person you would have her be, fulfilling your purpose for her life. Let me grow, too. Let me be a good parent.

Rosebud in the Snow

For everything created by God is good, and nothing is to be rejected if it is received with thanksgiving (1 Tim. 4:4).

"Joanna, Joanna." I whisper my new daughter's name as she lies sleeping on the bed beside me. How beautiful she looks, her soft pinkness in the white blanket like a rosebud in the snow. What a well-shaped head and ears and mouth. What long fingers. I touch each one. Will she grow up to be a musician — or an artist? No matter. What's important is that she be healthy.

Some women have uneasy moments during pregnancy, times when they are afraid. I used to lie awake sometimes in the night, asking myself, "What if the child I carry is less than whole? What would I do, Lord?"

But as in most cases, my fears were groundless. Today I remind myself of Jesus' advice that worry accomplishes nothing. And my faith grows.

I thank you, God, for this perfect baby.

Book Mother

Dear Lord, save me from being a "book mother." In my inexperience, don't let me turn into one of those women who expects her child to conform perfectly to the guidelines laid down in the plethora of information available on the subject of rearing babies. Right now I feel insecure and lacking in "motherly" feelings. It's all so new. Will I learn to be natural with this the joy of my life?

I want to enjoy my baby, to have fun with her, to establish a trusting relationship. Help me over these awkward first days, to listen to my instincts and common sense as well as to the experts. Lead me in love and tenderness as I explore this truly fascinating experience — parenthood. Joanna has come to us, a unique individual in your kingdom. I am grateful to you for the privilege of nurturing and guiding her growth. Don't let me make too many mistakes.

Rocking Chairs

He will not let your foot be moved, he who keeps you will not slumber (Ps. 121:3).

I'm convinced that what the world needs is more rocking chairs. Certainly every home with young children ought to have a rocking chair, a refuge to cuddle a child when she or he is sick, or afraid, or lonesome—a place for hugging and loving. Today even hospitals equip their maternity units with a rocking chair in each room so mothers may rock their newborn babies.

Our rocking chair came to us from my husband's family, handed along from one set of parents to the next. The arms are worn smooth, the seat is shiny from the movement of many bodies, the rockers are scuffed by the shoes of many feet. What stories it could tell. I would not trade this chair for elegant satin or brocade furniture costing many times its price. It's like a comfortable old friend. I depend on it.

Adults, too, need a "rocking chair," some place to retreat to for protection and warm love. Prayer is my rocking chair.

Lord, when I reach out to you in prayer, I feel comforted and confident, safe in the knowledge that you are listening and watching over me.

Tell God You Love Him

You shall love the Lord your God with all your heart, and with all your soul, and with all your mind (Matt. 22:37).

I've been "down" the past few weeks, and couldn't find the reason. My friends said, "It's only postpartum depression. Lots of women experience that. It will go away." But this is different, deeper. Something inside keeps me vaguely distressed, something is missing in my life. I, who bounce out of bed in the morning, and skip down the steps to peer out the front door with a "Good Morning, Lord," now go haltingly. Something is gone from my relationship with you, God.

In the middle of the night, when so many of my problems are solved, the answer came. I have been neglecting to say "I love you, O Lord." That has always been a daily part of my meditation, to express my love to the one who covers me so lavishly with his love. And my days have been hungry because of its absence.

Forgive me, Lord. You who know our inmost thinking, know that I love you with all my being, without my telling you. But I believe that you like to hear me say it. At least I feel uplifted and joyful when I say "I love you, O God, my redeemer."

Whistle at a Mother

Her children rise up and call her blessed; her hus-
band also, and he praises her (Prov. 31:28).

I have a friend who drives one of those big
"semi" rigs. When he cruises along city streets, he
makes a point of whistling at women pushing babies in strollers. "Ever since our second child arrived," he told me, "I've realized my wife felt that
her life was less than glamorous. Now my wife's
as cute a chick as you'll find anywhere, and I no-
ticed one day when a truck driver whistled at her
that, although she ignored him, her eyes sparkled
and she stood up a little straighter. Since then I've
been whistling at mothers."

When I got home, I put it to my wife. "Do you
consider it a compliment to be whistled at by truck
drivers when you're out with Joanna?" expecting
a haughty "no." My wife's pretty conservative, you
understand.

She grinned. "You bet I do! Although I stick
my nose in the air and look the other way, secretly
I'm flattered. If a truck driver whistles at me after
I've mopped the floor around Joanna's high chair
for the tenth time, straightened up with her cy-
clonic forays through the living room, and coped
with temper tantrums, I feel beautiful. Being whistled at by truck drivers is as American as apple
pie. It sure gives me a lift."

Dear Lord, help me be more perceptive of my
wife's needs. Show me how to be understanding
and warm with her.

A House Full of Smiles

For you shall go out in joy and be led forth in peace (Isa. 55:12).

Joanna smiled this morning! Not a vague reflex as before, but a deliberate controlled smile, crinkling her whole face, indeed engaging her entire body. New babies seem to smile with all their being, I discover in wonder. And so do I, in response. She recognizes me, and is happy that I am near her.

Suddenly the house, too, is wreathed in smiles. The furniture looks brighter, the plants in the window perkier, the sun a golden glow around us. How wonderfully you have planned for your little ones to grow and develop, Lord. And what joy surrounds a parent in these discoveries. I pray that my child may live out her life in joy, meeting challenges with a cheerful countenance.

Teach her to grow toward that inner peace that comes from the knowledge that your presence is always with us, guarding us. So that all her days she may dwell in a house full of smiles.

Getting Rid of Stress

Lo, sons are a heritage from the Lord, the fruit of the womb a reward (Ps. 127:3).

I did it! I'm soaking wet, but I gave Joanna her bath.

My wife, exercising great restraint, went off and left us alone, for which I thank her.

And we had fun. Joanna wiggled, and gurgled, and splashed — and laughed when I tickled her stomach with my hair. And amazingly, I found that all the tensions that had knotted me up today at work slipped down the drain with the bath water.

I must admit I wasn't eager to care for Joanna after a particularly stressful day. But I had promised. And now I'm glad. I heartily recommend bathing your youngster as a good way to get rid of butterflies in your stomach, and to get to know this new love in your life.

Dear God, I thank you for these joys of early parenthood, to be treasured and pulled out of our memory as we send our children off to school, college, and beyond.

Household of Faith

Now faith is the assurance of things hoped for, the conviction of things not seen (Heb. 11:1).

Joanna was baptized today, looking pure and peaceful in a christening dress first worn by my husband's mother. While the minister held her in his arms, repeating the well remembered phrases, she seemed very alert and knowing. This, I realize, is only a fond parent's prejudice, but forgivable, I think.

As the congregation rose and pledged its commitment to raise up this child in the "household of faith," the words kept ringing in my head.

It seems so simple to believe when one has grown up in a Christian family and church, surrounded by a "household of faith." But God knows this matter of faith in our individual lives is not so simple, and often elusive. Faith can be such a fragile thing, strong one minute, weak and fading away when we need most to trust God. The Bible is full of passages urging us to aim for a sincere faith, to stand firm in our faith, that there is power in faith, and that we can be saved through faith.

Increase my faith, O Lord, through all my days. And help my little child to come to the sure knowledge of salvation promised today in her baptism.

Baby Language

Let all that you do be done in love   (1 Cor. 16:14).

It's early morning. A car pulls out of the driveway next door, and a small voice floats through my bedroom window as I adjust my tie, preparing for my own drive to work. "Daddy, I love you!" The words bring a smile to me. Someday, I trust, Joanna will stand at the door, calling those same words to me. What a warm positive beginning for a father's workday.

In the meantime, I recognize that Joanna already has a "language" of sorts. We are now able to recognize her different cries, we know when she's hungry or in pain or signaling for attention. She gurgles and coos in response to our voices, and I've almost convinced my wife that at times Joanna is actually humming. Are these early signs that she'll grow up to be a singer? I dream.

O Lord, keep me sensitive to interpret correctly the language of my child as she grows. How tragic it is when adults and children fail to understand, when they talk past each other. Hold strong the bond of communication between us, help us to be open and loving in expressing our feelings, secure in the knowledge that your presence is always a bridge between us.

Through Baby's Eyes

For our knowledge is imperfect and prophecy is imperfect; but when the perfect comes, the imperfect will pass away (1 Cor. 13:9 – 10).

Joanna lies on her stomach on the carpet, energetically trying to roll over onto her back. There! She did it. I laugh and get down beside her, praising her lavishly. She, too, laughs and clutches my hair. I relax on the floor. How strange the room looks from this level — a maze of table and chair legs, and books. What must babies think as they view the world from this position? I glance up at the ceiling where a pool of sunlight dances to the shifting pattern of leaves outside. How utterly fascinating. Joanna also sees it, and the two of us watch for several minutes, absorbed in this television screen of nature.

Dear Lord, just as the baby's view of her physical world is imperfect, so is our adult inner view of life imperfect. Often we cannot see the direction we should follow; we are undecided and fearful. Should we accept that new job offer? Is this the time to add a room to the house? Are we equal to the added responsibility we've assumed at church? Speak to us, Lord. Assure us that as we pray and study the Bible and learn more about you, that our "baby eyes" will see more clearly and we shall live confidently in your light.

Good Morning, Lord

The earth, O Lord, is full of thy steadfast love; teach me thy statutes! (Ps. 119:64).

I love mornings, Lord. These days I awaken to the soft cooing of Joanna as she entertains herself in her bed. From my bedroom it sounds as if she is "talking," her voice taking on inflections in imitation of our adult voices. How marvelous is your plan for the attainment of language. I nestle for a few minutes under the covers, listening to other languages around me — the birds, the breeze, the chipmunk's "churck." How comforting is the language of nature, especially in the early morning when all is hushed and muffled, anticipating the sunrise over the trees.

Its energizing shaft touches my window. I rise quietly from my bed without disturbing my husband, and pad out to take up Joanna. "M-m-m," she sings and gurgles. Soundlessly, carrying my precious bundle, I make my way down the steps to open the front door. The sun is stretching across the lawn now. I stand motionless a few moments, savoring the beauty of another day beginning.

"Good morning," I whisper with a lilt in my voice. "Good morning, Lord."

Fill me this day with your goodness, Lord. Let it spread around me like the sun filtering across the lawn. Show me how to treat everyone I meet with the lavish love so evident in your natural world.

When God Bragged

Your wife will be like a fruitful vine within your house; your children will be like olive shoots around your table (Ps. 138:3).

Some of the most thrilling verses in the Bible are those in which God spoke directly to the men accompanying Jesus. I enjoy the account of Jesus' baptism in Matthew, when the Spirit of God descended like a dove and those around Jesus heard "a voice from heaven, saying 'This is my beloved Son, with whom I am well pleased'." Later when Jesus took Peter and James and John up into the mountain and became transformed, the voice from heaven said, "This is my beloved Son, with whom I am well pleased; listen to him."

Those were very human traits with which any parent can identify. It draws me closer to God to know that he, too, expressed pleasure and pride in his son. Of course, most parents spend far too much time sounding off to friends and relatives about the accomplishments and cute sayings of their children. But perhaps we can excuse ourselves, knowing that it is part of our nature to brag in this manner. After all, even God did not keep silent.

Winter Sun

Wait for the Lord; be strong, and let your heart take courage; yea, wait for the Lord! (Ps. 27:14).

The winter sun slants through the morning windows, wan and low and inadequate. It scarcely warms the spot on the rug where Joanna lies playing with her toes. Outside, two doves hug the earth with wings outspread, trying to soak up a little heat.

I sit at the table sipping coffee, listlessly leafing through the paper. We all seem to be waiting — waiting for the sun to regain its spring strength and brilliance, waiting for the earth to receive its vigor, waiting for a "turning of the clouds." It is the slack time in the life of our planet. Yet underneath, God, your miracles are quietly running on.

Just so, do you act in our inner natures, Lord. Sometimes it seems that we wait endlessly for answers to prayer, for you to guide us, to reinforce us. The way remains cloudy. Help us to know that through this seeming uncertainty, you are working, that your devoted love surrounds us, that at the proper time all things will come together for good. Give me patience to wait for spring.

Whistling at My Workbench

The carpenter stretches a line, he marks it out with a pencil; he fashions it with planes, and marks it with a compass (Isa. 44:13).

I remember how when I was very young I would hammer nails into boards while my father labored at his workbench in the garage. How proud I felt when he inspected and praised my finished product. As I became older, Dad taught me how to use more tools, and to respect the woodworking craft. He was a skilled craftsman, who patiently guided me into the pleasure and satisfaction of making things.

Today I began building a bed for Joanna to sleep in when she is older. My wife looks a bit alarmed. She has never seen me build something on this scale. But I am all confidence. Haven't I been planning this in secret almost from the beginning of her pregnancy? And quietly buying up the proper tools and wood? She'll see. I shall fashion a piece of furniture we can all be proud of. Perhaps even Joanna's child will sleep in this bed.

So I whistle and dream as I cut and measure and saw. My thoughts turn to another carpenter who once worked in his father's shop. Did Jesus also enjoy making things with his hands? A new kind of bond with the Master Carpenter makes this gift to Joanna even more precious.

Someone to Watch Over Me

I will live in them and move among them, and I will be their God, and they shall be my people (2 Cor. 6:16).

Joanna is already showing some signs of independence. She is handling a spoon, trying to feed herself, reaches for toys, and uses the furniture in a room to pull herself upright. These are delightful milestones for fond parents, evidences that our child is developing.

Surely one of the important goals of parents is to help their children grow into independent individuals, capable of thinking and acting responsibly on their own initiative. All of us can remember the thrill of accomplishment when we acted independently and successfully in childhood for the first time. We stood taller; it strengthened us to let go of parental supervision. And yet, how comforting it was to know that in the background someone was watching over us and protecting us. As an adult, I find just the opposite to be true. The *more* I depend on God, the stronger and freer I become.

The certainty that you are as close as my heartbeat, God, ready to support me when I ask, gives me the courage to try that new venture, to reach out to another person even at the risk of rebuff, to speak out against unfairness as I see it in my community.

God's Surprises

My heart is steadfast, O God ... I will sing and make melody (Ps. 57:7).

Usually I am an optimist. But some days when everything seems to go wrong, my sunny outlook on life fades. I kept telling myself today not to become discouraged. The day had to get better. Yet by dinner time I was frazzled and cranky. Then, as I was putting Joanna to bed, I saw a bright red bird perched on a tree branch outside her window. Suddenly it burst into song. Something inside me responded as my crabbiness was forgotten. What a refreshing, happy thing to end the day with a song!

The red bird taught me something about the joy of the unexpected. Often when we pray for help with a problem, we expect a certain solution and wait for that to happen. Sometimes we can't think of any answers to our problems, so we become depressed and anxious. Then God surprises us with a marvelous solution. If only we could pray with enough faith to ease all our tension and worry! Then our hearts and minds would be at perfect peace, even while God was working out an answer to our prayers.

Help me to remember the red bird in moments of confusion and despair, Lord. I want to trust you so much that even in times of trouble I can sing songs of praise.

The Need to Give

Give, and it will be given to you   (Luke 6:38).

I tuck Joanna in her crib and watch tenderly as she begins her nightly ritual of rocking on her elbows and knees. I smell her sweet baby scent and remember her smile. Softly I close the door and tiptoe down the stairs. I should feel exhausted from this day of baby tending — from feeding, changing, and bathing, to answering Joanna's constant demands for help and attention. Instead, I feel warm and nourished. Why, I ask myself. The answer comes to me even before I reach the living room. Today's busyness gave me so much joy because I gave so much of myself to someone else.

One of the very special rewards of motherhood surely must be giving to children who need and depend on them.

I believe this deep-seated desire to give to others, however, is not limited just to mothers. I believe all of us want to reach out to help others. Perhaps the way God freely offers himself to us is the basic impetus for our giving. At any rate, when we fail to extend ourselves, we soon feel as if our souls are wilting. Like plants in a spring rain, however, souls which give to others are nourished and blessed.

Thank you, Lord, for showing us the way.

Happy Feet

How beautiful upon the mountains are the feet of him who brings good tidings (Isa. 52:7).

It's almost time! Weekday mornings Joanna and I stop whatever we're doing at 9 o'clock and stroll down our driveway to greet children on their way to school. This is a big moment for Joanna. She waves and gurgles at the youngsters, and basks in their attention as they stop to say "hello."

With a soft pattering of feet, they trudge on. Some go skipping and hopping, eager for school. Others drag and scuff along reluctantly. Maybe they have tests today for which they feel poorly prepared, or maybe they are experiencing the pangs of being rejected by their peers.

Footsteps tell so much about us. When life is kind to us, when we hurt, when we feel defeated, these emotions are mirrored in our feet. Footsteps are as individual as signatures. I can certainly read my husband's state of mind in his footsteps. I remember how he came bouncing down the hall in the maternity unit where Joanna was born. That top-of-the-world feeling was evident in his every step. When I visited a friend in a nursing home, she called out to me before I entered her room. When I looked puzzled, she explained, "I recognized your footsteps. Your feet sound happy."

Does God Need Strokes?

Let the words of my mouth and the meditation of my heart be acceptable in thy sight, O Lord my rock and my redeemer (Ps. 19:14).

My bouncy "senior" neighbor stopped in today, "just to tell you what a fantastic mother I think you are," she said, all smiles and chucking Joanna under the chin. "I was a long time feeling comfortable with my three. Already you've achieved a loving calm relationship." What a day brightener for me!

Most of us have a very hungry desire to be told we are doing something well, to be complimented, to be "stroked" once in awhile. It's not enough to be satisfied within ourselves that we have done our best; we want to be acknowledged by others. I know that I melt like warm butter under a friend's praise, and vow in turn to be more vocal in praising others. Such strokes make the world a kinder place.

I wonder — does God ever feel the need of strokes? I know that when I praise him and thank him for his goodness to me, I feel exalted. Is this partly because he is pleased to have me tell him so? Can it be that I am uplifted because God is glad to hear my prayers? I'm not sure. But a stirring inside me compels me to continue to worship God and magnify his name.

Mirror, Mirror

But who can discern his errors? Clear thou me from hidden faults (Ps. 19:12).

Joanna has found a new toy — the mirror in the hallway door. It is providing us all with many moments of fun and play. Joanna examines and pats the baby in the glass, "talks" to her, smiles and grows excited, while we peek unnoticed from the doorway. She also likes to be held in front of the mirror. At first she seemed puzzled by this "mirror mother" talking while her voice came from behind. But quicker than we expected she grasped the idea of mirror images, and now she loves to imitate our expressions.

I suppose many adults also indulge in mirror play, at least surreptitiously. I know that I check my hairdo or shirttail as I pass reflections in a store window and find myself start to smile if I catch a frowning look on my face in shopping mall mirrors. Sometimes I gaze searchingly at my mirror image. Does my character show in my face?

If only there were a mirror that accurately revealed our inner nature to us. We think we know ourselves, but in truth all our lives we are discovering things about ourselves, new strengths, new weaknesses we were not conscious of.

I am constantly surprising myself, Lord, in self-knowledge. Help me to keep growing toward the person you have planned for me to be. Especially show me my hidden sins and failures so that I may deal with them.

When I Hurt

Is any one among you suffering? Let him pray (James 5:13).

Even the best marriages have times of misunderstanding, anger, and hurt. I'm feeling some hurt and anger right this moment. Something my husband said to me last night unintentionally hurt me deeply. I wanted to lash back at him with some cruel words of my own, but fortunately I was speechless. I charged out to the kitchen instead, and rattled around some pots and pans rather enthusiastically as I started dinner.

Today I want to shut myself away and nurse my hurt. That won't do. If I don't say anything, my husband won't know what is bothering me. Still, can I tell him what is on my mind without either causing him pain or making him feel guilty? How I can talk to him without becoming too emotional? Help me, Lord, to find the right words. Help me to speak with compassion and love as well as honesty.

Talking over our hurts with you usually takes the sting out of them, Lord. Will my talk with you also, in some way, prepare my husband for the talk we must have?

Think Happy

But grow in the grace and knowledge of our Lord and Savior Jesus Christ. To him be the glory both now and to the day of eternity. Amen.
(2 Peter 3:18).

On a beautiful morning like this one, it's easy to see God everywhere. The sunrise, the sweet air, the paperboy grinning as he hands me the paper. Oh, I love to be up early and savor your good earth, God. Help me keep this feeling all day long. Help me to think happy.

It's so easy to become pessimistic about the noisy neighbor, about world affairs, about the future. What a lack of faith that shows. Don't let me be that way. Let me look at my child growing healthy and lovely. Let me look at my husband so full of confidence. Fill my cup with love so that it spills over to everyone I meet.

Remind me that you work through other people, too. Let me see you shining through their lives. Help me see down the long road toward universal harmony and peace. Let me do my part in making it come true. Let me think happy all my life.

A Cup of Kindness

The fruit of the Spirit is love, joy, peace, patience, kindness, goodness, faithfulness (Gal. 5:22).

Today people have been especially kind to me. I tend to expect that sort of thing from friends, but hardly from strangers. Yet a station attendant volunteered to pump gas for me at the self-serve island, saying he wasn't busy, and a customer in line at the bank let me go ahead of her when Joanna became fussy.

I started day-dreaming about a world where kindness would become a habitual way of life. Why not? If people used the same amount of energy to show acts of kindness that they normally expended in selfishness, violence, and vandalism — how quickly all men might be united in brotherhood. I remember what my mother's aunt once said to us at an annual family reunion. "Not all of you can grow up to be pretty, rich, or athletic, but you can all be kind. Pass along a cup of kindness to everyone you meet," she suggested, "and I promise you'll have more friends than you know what to do with."

Kindness means thinking about others and becoming sensitive to their needs. That's where we often fail — we're so wrapped up in our own affairs that we don't take time to hear another person's cry.

Change our hearts, Lord. Help us to remember how kind you are to us, so that out of gratitude we can show kindness to others.

Summer Specials

They shall not hurt or destroy in all my holy mountain; for the earth shall be full of the knowledge of the Lord (Isa. 11:9).

We are conditioned to thinking of "summer specials" as merchandise reduced in price by merchants traditionally moving out their summer stock, so that the term means little else to us today. But I propose that some of the best "summer specials" to be had are picnics.

In my part of the country, with four distinct seasons, summer is a time for picnics. Some of my fondest childhood memories revolve around picnics — family reunions, huge Fourth of July picnics for the entire community, spur-of-the-moment picnics we children enjoyed, taking sandwiches down to the bank of a stream not far away. Usually a few dogs trailed along, managing to wet us thoroughly to our delight, as they splashed in the water.

We took Joanna on her first picnic yesterday, to a quiet area not far from a lake. To lie on warm grass and make pictures in the clouds is more therapeutic than a psychiatrist's couch any day. Breathing sweet air, watching the movement of birds while they dart busily, I am aware of the peace, harmony, and oneness of this world you have planned so perfectly and lovingly, dear God.

In Praise of Grandparents

The teaching of the wise is a fountain of life (Prov. 13:14).

One of God's brightest blessings to us is the blessing of grandparents. We are especially grateful that all four of Joanna's grandparents live close by. People who are parents, yet freed from parental responsibilities, are often eager to spend time with children. They play with them, listen to them, and tell them stories about the past. They also teach them valuable lessons on how to live and what to believe. We are fortunate Joanna's grandparents can be with her so often.

She already knows each one of them, and smiles when she sees them. She also "talks" her own special language to them, trying to communicate how happy she is to be with them. I foresee many future hours of walks, trips the zoo, and rides on the playground. Grandparents are a significant part of our family circle.

Some children do not have grandparents they can visit. Perhaps their parents should seek out an elderly couple who might be eager to fill this void. Such relationships could bring immeasureable joy to children as well as their adopted "grandparents." Each generation of God's people has much to share with the next one.

Faltering Minds

I have seen his ways, but I will heal him; I will lead him and requite him with comfort (Isa. 57:18).

I feel as if I have failed, Lord. Our church family has watched helplessly as one of our members drifts away from normal behavior these past few months. What can we do to help him more? Some of us have found him places to live, but after a few days he leaves. We make arrangements for him to see professional counselors, he refuses to keep the appointments. Still, he spends a lot of time wandering around our church. Does it still represent a kind of refuge for him?

Carl and I had a pleasant casual friendship. We served on several church committees together. I feel a responsibility for him, and have tried to talk to him. I have listened to his problems and have loaned him money. Yet all these efforts seem to have failed. My brother continues to drift away.

Why, Lord, do some of your children wander away from those who care about them? Is this man drifting because of something I have failed to understand? Open my mind and heart, Lord. And if I cannot reach him, lay your healing hand on him through someone else.

Talk to Me

Think over what I say, for the Lord will grant you understanding in everything (2 Tim. 2:7).

Child development experts urge parents to talk a lot to their babies. This is the way baby learns to talk. Joanna thinks it great fun for us to repeat all the sounds she makes as she runs through her repertoire. And she delights in having us recite nursery rhymes. She also takes pleasure in "talking" to the tinkling windchime on the porch, much to our amusement. How wonderful it is to have someone to talk to you. Surely one of the lonelinesses of living by oneself is having no one to share conversation.

I think that's why many people keep the radio or television set turned on much of the time. They long for the sound of another person's voice. The telephone is a boon for alleviating loneliness. Our friend, a receptionist at one of the local television stations, tells us that several women frequently call her. "I can tell they don't want any specific information," she says. "They're just lonely and have no one to talk to. So I try to spend a little time with each one if my board is not too busy."

In the same way, we grow lonely to talk to you, God. It's easy to call your number. We have only to open the Bible and start reading. If we query "How am I to live? What are you like, God?" you will answer us in the Bible.

How to Get Rid of Loneliness

On the day I called, thou didst answer me, my strength of soul thou didst increase (Ps. 138:3).

Taking care of a baby is often a lonely job. Joanna is adorable, but all her smiles, tears, and baby talk can't substitute for communication with other adults. Day after day I find myself yearning for someone to exchange thoughts and opinions with, and day after day I feel increasingly more fenced in. I may be a mother, but I am also a person who needs mental stimulation. How can I overcome this overwhelming feeling of loneliness?

God gave me an answer. It was so simple that at first I ignored it. Yet the idea was persistent. "Do something for someone else who is lonely." I sat down and made out a list to put right next to the telephone. The list included the names of people who could use a friendly phone call, a cheery little letter, or even a warm invitation to lunch. It even included the names of neighbors who might want me to take them shopping. Now my agenda which includes both adults and Joanna is full.

Thank you, Lord, for showing me how to get rid of loneliness. I know that I am never really alone and that you walk beside me. Yet you are also aware of my needs and have showed me how to meet them.

Heroes

Arise and shine; for your light has come, and the glory of the Lord has risen upon you (Isa. 60:1).

Whatever happened to heroes? I remember my father telling with shining eyes about the athletes and characters in books he admired as a child. Those people were as real to him as his own neighbors. He said that at one time he even went around calling himself "David" after the Old Testament shepherd and king.

We don't talk much about heroes today, don't use the term in referring to outstanding people. Is it because we are inclined to see their faults right along with their accomplishments, and this tempers our esteem? Does this dampen our enthusiasm and prevent us from using them as role models for ourselves as well as for our children? I hope not. We all need heroes to look up to.

I want Joanna to find heroes, strong people to model her behavior after — perhaps a Bible character, perhaps an Olympic ice-skater, a third-grade teacher, or a lovely neighbor down the street. Just ordinary people with a touch of greatness.

Certainly one of the lessons of the Bible is that God uses ordinary people to perform extraordinary tasks. Heroes still live among us, people who can inspire us to exert our best efforts.

Open our eyes, Lord, to the heroes of our time.

Listening

The Lord will rescue me from every evil and save me for his heavenly kingdom. (2 Tim. 4:18).

It is dusk and a soft rain fails, imparting a lulling "swish" sound to the tires of passing cars, carrying people home from work. But my ears strain for the sound of one particular car that will bring my husband back to me from his job. I look forward to our cozy evenings together, a time to exchange tidbits from our day, to share confidences and aspirations. I feed Joanna and begin dinner preparation. But always a part of my mind is listening, waiting for the familiar sound.

I turn on lights around the house. The hour grows late. Where can he be? Is he all right? With so many automobile accidents happening . . . Fear snatches my heart. I pace the living room, glance out the front door a dozen times, return to the kitchen to check the stew. Then I hear the peculiar "thump" our car makes as it turns in the driveway, and a faint "toot" on the horn. My heart leaps within me. God has led my husband home safely after his day's traveling. Oh, thank you, God!

Help me, God, to trust, to know that you travel the way with each of us all day, that you guard us and keep us from harm.

Aching Arms

Thy rod and thy staff, they comfort me   (Ps. 23:4).

Our friends lost their baby last night. His heart was damaged and he lived only a few hours. His parents are devastated. What can we say to them? How can we comfort them, Lord?

One is never prepared for such a circumstance. How heartbreaking it must be to come back to a home ready with tiny new clothes and a waiting cradle. Anything we might say to them sounds inadequate. We cannot suggest that God will someday give them other children. They wanted *this* one, Lord.

There are so many things in life that we can't understand, so many mysteries. Sometimes we must simply follow you in faith through dark valleys, trusting that things will come right in the sweep of time.

Our own baby sleeps sweetly in the next room. Tell us, Lord, what we should say to Carol and Bob.

Faces

For behold, the kingdom of God is in the midst of you (Luke 17:21).

Joanna has become fascinated with faces. She is continually poking her fingers in our eyes, nose, and mouth. She grabs our hair and ears — and forgets to let go. Ditto with glasses. The entire family finds this a bit disconcerting, and hopes this phase will not last too long. We tell ourselves this is her way of learning more about us.

I can appreciate Joanna's curiosity. In all the world no two faces are exactly alike, even among twins. In a crowd I often look at people around me, wondering what they are like behind this mask we call face. Are they happy? Are they afraid? Are they coping courageously with some serious problem? But all too soon, my attention is caught elsewhere, and the faces melt back into an anonymous montage. They lose their focus. Even among people I see frequently — the bank teller, the grocery clerk — I often don't look at them with seeing eyes. I "see but do not perceive."

Dear Lord, teach me to look with gentle understanding at the persons you've placed about me. Let me be tuned in to their inner nature, to sense when they need a sympathetic smile or a pat on the back. Let your love which binds us all together flow between us, so that the other persons know I am glad you brought us together.

Coming and Going

And when I go and prepare a place for you, I will come again and will take you to myself, that where I am you may be also (John 14:3).

She's gone, this gracious friend, leaving echoes in our hearts of her sweet voice and gentle ways. She was a newspaper woman, a columnist, bringing to her writing a compassion and respect for commitment that will be missed by the entire community. Very few of her readers knew that she viewed the world from a wheelchair and that her observations and writings grew out of what she saw from her picture window or resulted from her skill on the telephone. Her cheerful optimism was catching, and I always felt uplifted after a conversation with her.

In these moments, Lord, while I hold Joanna on my lap, so freshly come to this world, the mystery of life and death and my questions about them are close to the surface. Help me to approach them without fear. For, in truth, we do but pass through here into another realm. Show me how to live with assurance and greet each day with enthusiasm.

Explaining God

One generation shall laud thy works to another, and shall declare thy mighty acts (Ps. 145:4).

Some day Joanna will climb up in my lap and say, "Daddy, tell me about God." What am I going to say to her? How can I possibly tell her the right things that will encourage her to walk in the ways of the Lord? How can I show her how much faith in God means to me? I don't want to fail her — or you, Lord. Yet I am afraid of this awesome responsibility.

I tell myself godly parents have been succeeding for thousands of generations. I remind myself of the Christian convictions I learned from my own parents: that you are a God of love who seeks us out so that we learn to love you back; that you are always with us to share our hurts, our troubles, and our good times; and that you rejoice when our hearts and lives are filled with joy. I remember how I learned that prayer opens the door to our souls so that your divine power can work its will within us, and how praise and thanks for all the good things you give us makes our days richer.

I learned all this from my parents. I can pick each teaching up, one at a time, like tools from my workbench, to begin teaching Joanna. We will learn together a process that is never finished.

Rainbows

For the promise is to you and to your children and to all that are far off   (Acts 2:39).

A rainbow graced the sky this afternoon. As a summer shower passed over, the sun came out, growing in intensity, so that a beautiful brilliant arch rose in the eastern sky. Not one but two rainbows appeared, sending a thrill of delight through me.

For I still find magic in rainbows. Such a promise, God, as if you were saying, "See how beautiful my world can be? Come, pause a moment, think of all the good things in your life. Be filled with joy!"

Sometimes I think God sends his Holy Spirit to us like a rainbow. I used to find the Holy Spirit concept puzzling. But not any more. Inside, I can see it curving down from God to each one of us, touching us with the promise of life filled with his presence.

Will Joanna love rainbows the way I do? Shall I hang a little glass rainbow in her window to catch the sun until the day when I can explain its real promise to her?

Hug a Tree

God saw everything that he had made, and behold it was very good (Gen. 1:31).

We planted a tree for Joanna this morning. It's a sturdy apple tree, the largest we could afford. A lot of memories came to me as we spread the roots and tamped earth around them. I especially thought of the old June apple tree I played in when I was a child.

That old tree was more than a tree. It was a castle, a spaceship, cave, or whatever else my friends and I wanted it to be. Later it became my haven for reading or getting away by myself so I could think, make plans, or just dream. I can recall even today its warm scratchy bark, its sweet-tart fruit, and the safe contentment I felt when I rested on its limbs. Sometimes even now, when we visit my parents, I walk out to the old tree and wrap my arms around its trunk, and breathe in its rich, woodsy aroma. "My old friend," I murmur.

Will Joanna feel this way someday about the apple tree we planted today? I hope so. The natural world *is* our friend, and we should take time to explore and respect and protect it. We need to lie among the daisies, watch the rabbits at dusk, to treat gently and lovingly this beautiful but vulnerable world you have given us, Lord.

A Circle of Music

For he is gracious and a song of praise is seemly
(Ps. 147:1).

All my life I have been surrounded by music. Not just by stereo recordings, radio, and live concerts, but music from outdoors as well. My childhood was spent only two blocks from the church we attended. Every day at noon and six PM the church carillon played a series of hymns. I learned to sing them all. Most mothers in the neighborhood instructed their children to come home for lunch when the carillon played. In the evening, my family sat down to dinner accompanied by its sweet background.

Today we live near a university that boasts a majestic carillon tower. We hear familiar songs in the evening and a refrain from our state song on the hour. Visiting carilloneers often share their skill for our enjoyment.

What a blessing is music in our lives. How pleasant to let the cares of the day slip away as we relax in the melody and harmony of song.

Lord, fill my life with your song.

Rejection Slips

The Lord is my helper, I will not be afraid
(Heb. 13:6).

I sent off my first manuscript to a magazine publisher. Great hope and fear winged along with it, hope that the publisher would purchase it, fear at the thought that he/she would return the piece. Now I sit at my desk holding in my hands the returned manuscript, reading and rereading the pink rejection slip that accompanied it. My shoulders slump dejectedly, my heart plummets down around my ankles. I feel rejected in my entire being.

But then I remember that life is filled with risk-taking. Many times we expose ourselves to the rejection of others in what we do. Changing jobs, trying a different approach with our children, or even extending ourselves to strangers, all involve elements of risk. But God "did not give us a spirit of timidity," but instead a "spirit of power and love and self-control." When we feel right about doing something or when a plan keeps coming back to us, I believe that God is nudging us to go ahead.

Why get worried about one rejection from one publisher? I'll send it off to another. Thank you, Lord, for giving me the courage to try again.

First Tooth

The Lord is near to the brokenhearted, and saves the crushed in spirit (Ps. 34:18).

An event! Joanna cut her first tooth today. We've been expecting it, rubbing her hot and swollen gums, wishing it along. This morning it appeared, perfect and pearllike! What an amazing seven months this has been. Joanna's eyes and hearing are now almost fully developed, she responds to us with smiles, and shows her pleasure in being with us. She is beginning to make deliberate sounds of "talking" and expects us to respond in the same language. She is finding some skill with her hands. Reaching, holding, and tugging are better coordinated. Her big problem at the moment is in letting go! How satisfying are the rewards of living with a beautiful developing child.

I think you must look with joy on the homes where children are growing according to your plan, Lord. But what about the children without homes? What about those little ones left without parents, with no one to exclaim over a first tooth? Oh, spread your mantle of special love and care over these less fortunate. Bring together those children and adults eager to adopt them. Show my husband and me how to encourage some wavering friends to embark on the fulfilling joy of adoption.

Make a Good Day

Thou hast turned for me my mourning into dancing; thou has loosed my sackcloth and girded me with gladness (Ps. 30:11).

"Have a good day."

This casual phrase runs like a litany through our day of chance contacts with people at the grocery store, the drug store, and even the gas station. Everyone we meet seems to be wishing us well.

"Completely false," says my neighbor across the street.

"I'm surfeited with these superficial meaningless expressions," growls my English professor friend.

Perhaps. Yet every time I hear "Have a good day," I notice the smile and direct eye contact that goes with it. I feel warm and friendly, even when I suspect the phrase is automatic. Underneath, I detect a genuine feeling of courtesy and good will.

This morning a van cruised down my street with an updated version of the old cliche. "*Make a good day*" was written across its spare tire. What an optimistic outlook. It made me vow to start every day armed with the knowledge of God's steadfast love and strength, and *make* a good day.

Saturday Morning Breakfast

And the effect of righteousness will be peace, and the result of righteousness quietness and trust for ever (Isa. 32:17).

Saturday morning breakfast in what we grandly call our "garden room" is a pleasant interlude in our household. While my wife prepares the meal, I help by taking charge of Joanna as she bustles around, crawling, pulling herself up against the furniture, banging toys, and chattering all the time. We settle down to read the paper, sharing tidbits of news with each other, watching the birds drop down for a drink at our fountain, admiring our tomato crop hanging plump on the vines. Some mornings a visiting musician plays a cascade of melody on the university carillon not far away. I am as happy as a king at peace in his kingdom.

It's easy to envision a world of peace on Saturday mornings, Lord. All the world is aching for peace. Will mine be the generation to achieve it? Can the swell of mankind today reaching toward more righteousness bring an end to war for all time? This is my prayer, God, on this Saturday morning, that the individuals living by your will shall multiply until all the earth is covered with the bright aura of peace.

Squashed Peas

Love is patient and kind (1 Cor. 13:4).

Ever since Joanna has been sitting in a high chair and attempting to feed herself, one end of the kitchen looks like an upturned salad bowl. Eating has become high adventure for her, to be accompanied by gleeful mashing, squeezing, and smearing of food. Her spoon she wields with the aplomb of an orchestra conductor, scattering food with cheerful abandonment. I'm forever scooping up squashed peas off the floor, while pieces of banana, toast, and orange plop in a steady shower over the rim of her tray. "Is she getting enough nourishment?" I fret.

"Don't worry," soothes the doctor.

"Will she grow out of this messy stage soon?" I pout.

"Probably not," is his discouraging reply.

I heave a deep sigh, determined that I will exhibit more patience, and that I am learning with bowed head. Oops, there goes another pea. Got it!

Remind, me dear God, you who are so very patient with me, that, like children and adults, babies are not 100 percent perfect all the time. Let me learn patience, lots of it —and soon!

A Helping Hand

A brother helped is like a strong city   (Prov. 18:19a).

As I push Joanna in her stroller down the sidewalk in my neighborhood, I am diverted from watching Joanna's hands and legs performing aerobics by the number of houses which display a large red hand in a front window. The Helping Hand project it's called, according to my wife, a signal to school children that inside they can find assistance and shelter if they need it.

I am reminded of good people everywhere who wear invisible Helping Hands, stretching out their loving care to others. In church last night, for instance, I listened to a missionary doctor speak about her work in a hospital in the bush country of Zaire. She lives out her life in calm dedication to people ignored by their own government. She speaks of roads made impassable by the rainy season, of medicines stolen from mailed packages, of black market gasoline purchased to run hospital generators. Defying these problems, she laughs and shines as one who is satisfied with her choice.

O Lord, how happy are those who reach out to others. Make me aware of the needs of people around me, and guide my hands to help them.

Cruising

But if we hope for what we do not see, we wait for it with patience   (Rom. 8:25).

Joanna is getting ready to walk. She pulls herself to a standing position in her playpen, then seems to forget to hold on to the sides as she examines a toy. She also moves around the room by grabbing different pieces of furniture. The doctor calls this "cruising."

I wish I could be more patient with the cruising stage of learning. Right now I'm trying to learn to crochet. Although my goal is to make an afghan for Joanna's bed, I wisely began in a small way with a scarf. Tonight while we watched television, I felt so smug doing two things at once, but found my scarf was growing wider with every turn of the rows. Now I shall have to go back to square one. All of which points up that there is a lot of testing and experimenting for me in learning.

I think that I'm like that in my spiritual progress, too, Lord. Sometimes when I read of religious leaders who have had a one-time experience which sets them firmly on a high spiritual plane, I say "What's the matter with me? Why doesn't my path unfold with such clarity?" My scarf experience tells me that in all my learning there will be a lot of cruising, Lord.

For Amber Waves of Grain

*Put in your sickle, and reap, for the hour to reap
has come, for the harvest of the earth is fully ripe
(Rev. 14:15).*

We bundled Joanna into her stroller today, and
took off for the State Fair. I've loved fairs ever
since I won a 4-H ribbon for my butterfly collec-
tion in the fourth grade. My wife, to my surprise,
enjoys fairs almost as much as I do. These great
"show-and-tell" events offer something for everyone to enjoy.

This year we saw were an impressive furnished
replica of the White House and a pioneer village
where occupants worked with tools of an earlier
period. How ingenous is the mind of men! But
always my favorite exhibit is the display of prize-
winning produce grown on farms in our area.
Viewing the rows and rows of luscious tomatoes,
apples, "biggest" squash, "tallest" corn, and piles
of melons, I am overwhelmed with thoughts of
man's dedicated work and God's bounty in providing for us. As I gaze over this abundant cornuco-
pia, I feel like getting down on my knees in grateful
prayer to God for his lavish providence.

Thank you, Lord, for blessing our harvest.

Feeling Creamy

Thou preparest a table before me in the presence of my enemies; thou anointest my head with oil, my cup overflows (Ps. 23:5).

I have a friend who grew up on a farm who always says she's feeling "creamy" when she's had a good day. "You know," she says with a grin, "a day when, like cream, you just naturally rise to the top of the milk." That's the way I feel today, Lord, right on top of the milk!

When I was a teenager, I expected that if I were a good Christian, then everything would go right all the time — all my decisions would be the right ones, I would have no problems, and I would float euphorically through life. Somehow, I reasoned, when life turned sour, I had failed God. Now I know better. The Christian does not escape all troubles. We have to face the very same problems in life that non-Christians have to face. The difference is in knowing that God surrounds us with his love at all times, understanding that he is beside us, nurturing us, showing us the way out of our troubles.

Under his care, we can experience peace so deep and satisfying that the troubles have no power to overwhelm us. We can rise to the top of the milk and feel creamy!

Stepping Out Alone

Seek the Lord and his strength, seek his presence continually (Ps. 105:4).

Our little girl is walking! Last night she finally let go of the edge of a low table, and with her daddy's coaxing took her first steps into his waiting arms. We, of course, immediately got on the phone to tell the grandparents, and then we got out the camera to take pictures of her second "solo" walk. Today Joanna can't get enough of this new mode of transportation, and she is managing to tire us all with her efforts. Each time she takes steps away from a piece of furniture, we are waiting to catch her with open arms and a big smile.

Would Joanna have learned to walk this early if her father's loving arms had not been there to catch her? Did the fact that she trusted him encourage her to try her first steps?

All through life we are faced with stepping out alone. It takes courage to leave the old and embrace the unfamiliar. Often we become fearful; like Peter we falter at walking on the water. How reassuring it is to know that whenever we take our first steps into unknown waters, God's loving arms are stretched out wide to catch us.

Kitchen Play

Serve the Lord with gladness   (Ps. 100:2).

If Joanna could talk, I'm sure she would say the kitchen is her favorite room in our house. Partly it's because I spend so much time "playing" there and partly it's because she is fascinated with all the drawers and cupboards waiting to be explored—and emptied. With great concentration she investigates each one. I've tried putting unbreakable articles in one cupboard and encouraging her to play there. But every mother knows this is only a temporary diversion. Soon Joanna is banging her way along the row of cupboards. Out comes everything. If I'm lucky, she'll put everything back, though not necessarily in the same cupboard. That this is unproductive bothers her not at all.

As I watch her busy amid the clutter, I am suddenly reminded of adults whose lives are as cluttered and unproductive as Joanna's kitchen exercises. I think especially of two couples we know who spend their time rushing from one "fun" engagement to another, always busy, filling their days with "kitchen play." Once in awhile they look a little desperate as they vaguely sense they are missing the heart of life.

I am convinced that our purpose here on earth is not to keep busy, but to serve you, O Lord. Is there some way I can help my friends see this? I'm listening.

Speed Calling

Incline thy ear to me; answer me speedily in the day when I call (Ps. 102:2).

The telephone company recently sent us a brochure offering us a new service named "speed calling." When emergencies happen at home, the brochure explains, you can get help faster by dialing one or two digits instead of seven. It's a good idea, I think, especially for handicapped and elderly people.

The special service got me thinking about how convenient it is to call God. No-digit prayer is our hotline to God, if and when crises occur, and day-by-day communication on an open line with him assures us that he is always willing to listen to us.

Think of how important prayer is in our lives. Frequent communication with God lifts our burdens, meets our needs, and enriches our lives. Talking to him eases our fears, and shakes us loose from negative thoughts. Prayer assures us that God is always near us and is willing to talk to us.

Thank you, God, for answering every one of our speed calls to you.

Curiouser and Curiouser

Thou knowest me right well; my frame was not hidden from thee, when I was being made in secret (Ps. 139:15).

As in Lewis Carrolls's *Alice in Wonderland*, babies seem to find life curiouser and curiouser as they grow. It is God's way of helping them learn about their world, and an important part of their development. Joanna at nine months is determined to grab, poke, taste, and throw everything within her grasp. Curiosity is a real driving force in her life. Joanna is changing from a helpless infant into an active, thinking human being, and we are sometimes amazed at her inventiveness in reaching objects she covets. I hope she will always remain curious about life around her.

Curiosity leads us to explore and learn and create. And curiosity about our spiritual life, I think is refreshing to God. It's all right to question and wonder about God and his power in our lives. Some of us go through an intensive seeking and even doubting at some period in our lives. I believe God doesn't mind. He knows this is one way we gain better understanding of him and stretch our faith. Religious curiosity is a healthy thing.

Lady with the Red Bow

In quietness and in trust shall be your strength (Isa. 30:15).

I notice her out of the corner of my eye, making her way carefully along the sidewalk as I ease my car to a stop at the intersection. Stooped, wearing a sweater, in one hand she clutches the trademark of women her age, a large shopping bag. She stops cautiously at the corner. "Just another elderly grey-haired lady passing by on her trip to the grocery," I think. But no. Wait. There is a difference here. Something about this lady brings me a smile and a chuckle, lifting my spirits. For nodding gaily among her curls, perches a brave red bow. I could cheer.

What an optimist she must be, asserting her confidence in the day with this bright talisman. I should like to know her, this lady with the red bow. As she steps down off the curb, she waves and smiles at Joanna strapped in her car seat. Does she have grandchildren, I wonder? If so, how enriched they must be. Grandparents, too, are an important part of the family circle.

Help me remember, Lord, to mail off pictures of Joanna to her grandparents today. And be tender with this lady with the red bow.

Laugh at the Devil

Resist the devil and he will flee from you
(James 4:7).

What do you think the devil looks like? Some
of my friends picture him as the cartoon character
who is dressed in red, has horns sticking out of
his head, and carries a long pitchfork. Some people think of Satan as a huge weight they carry on
their back. Others describe him in terms of terror
or fear. I think of Satan as a dark, gloomy shape
that sneers at me. Sometimes it looms like a giant
above me, and sometimes it just sits next to me
like a constant, irritating little pest. Regardless of
its size, this evil presence which urges us into
temptation, is not someone to be taken lightly. He
is so powerful that even Jesus suffered temptation
at his hands. Jesus resisted the devil, of course,
but how can we, in our weakness, resist him?

We must, first of all, turn our thoughts away
from temptation, and focus on God. James says,
"Draw near to God and he will draw near to you."
He also says that if you lack wisdom, you should
ask God for help and he will give it to you. God
is more powerful than the devil, so thoughts about
him are stronger than thoughts about doing evil.
Armed with this promise, I have found that I can
laugh both at the dark giant above me and the
small pest beside me. Both of them vanish when
they discover I am no longer afraid of what they
can do to one who is in God's hands.

Mountains of Laundry

I can do all things in him who strengthens me
(Phil. 4:13).

I'm tired, Lord, too tired to get out of this chair.
I need a push to get through the rest of the day.
Joanna has been fussy with a cold, has trouble
keeping down her food, and I've a mountain of
laundry to fold and put away.

I feel defeated and discouraged, I hate the seem-
ingly endless round of activities that fill my life
right now — washing, cleaning, shopping. I can't
get organized these days. There's never enough
time for the creative things I used to do. My life
is one long series of interruptions. I want more
freedom!

Thank you, Lord, for letting me sound off this
way. I feel better already. I would feel guilty expressing these emotions to anyone else. But you
understand. You sense it is just a momentary
weakness. You know that I am totally absorbed in
this life you have given us to love, that Joanna is
the joy of our lives. Lift me up, strengthen me.
Help me over this hurdle of defeat, so that I may
finish out the day with a singing heart.

Butterflies in the Garden

Then will I go to the altar of God, to God my exceeding joy (Ps. 43:4).

You can tell summer is waning. Joanna and I saw our first butterflies in the garden this morning. Two exhuberant yellow swallowtails danced a ballet over the lantana bush, sipping nectar. They were so close, I could almost touch their fragile beauty. Joanna seemed enchanted with their motion. We both sat transfixed, delighted by one of God's small miracles.

To the Chinese people the butterfly is a symbol of joy, to Christians it sometimes speaks of resurrection. However we view it, the butterfly conjurs up a vision of loveliness. Would that it could linger with us longer. But though its life span is short, the butterfly acts out its purpose in God's kingdom, disappears, and leaves behind it the seeds of a new cycle.

I think sometimes that our human lives are like butterflies. We are shocked and saddened when a life is snuffed out early. But who are we to say that serving God requires a long life? The loving deeds that a person leaves behind cannot be measured in years. Does it really matter how long it takes to complete our individual purpose on earth?

Dear God, go with me each day. May I dance the joyful dance of the butterfly in accomplishing your plans for my life. Whether the days be long or short matters not.

First Shoes

And which of you by being anxious can add a cubit to his span of life? (Luke 12:25).

Joanna is wearing her first pair of shoes, and is delighted with these "new toys". She has devoted half the day to stomping in them on the tiles in front of the fireplace, and the other half to untying the laces. And I? I find myself feeling a little sad, to my chagrin. I, too, ought to be delighted. But I have discovered there's something symbolic about buying my child her first pair of shoes. In a way, it is the first tangible evidence that this child of mine is beginning to grow away from me, ever so slightly. No longer will baby feet pound and knead my stomach as I hold her. Almost left behind is her game of playing with her toes. Joanna has arrived in the upright world and strides forth confidently to explore it by herself, leaving me to wonder where the baby days have flown.

But it will be this way all our days of living together. I am glad for Joanna to take these independent steps, and yet anxious. I want to protect her; I don't want my child to be hurt by life. I know I cannot smooth all the paths before her. But she is such a tender flower right now. Then I remember someone said, "Let go and let God," and pause.

You, Lord, will watch over my child. I commit Joanna to your hands, assured and unafraid. I know that I will pray this prayer many times in the years to come: Help me, O Lord, to let go and let you take over.

Try a Prayer Break

Come away by yourselves ... and rest a while (Mark 6:31).

In the hectic pace of modern life, the coffee break has become an established custom in most offices and business places. Getting up from a desk or laying down tools for a few minutes sends us back to work with renewed energy and a fresh outlook. At home, too, a trip to the kitchen for a cup of coffee and a lingering glance out the window makes a pleasant change in activity.

Have you ever tried a prayer break during the day? Quick moments of communion with God can lift your spirit and remind you that he is here now, moving beside you. You don't need to go to a special place for prayer. You can pray while you're driving the car, walking from the bus, waiting in line at the post office. We have so many blessings to praise God for that we could spend the whole day counting them. Try naming a few for a pick-me-up.

Sometimes when I stand in line at the grocery check-out counter, I pray for the other people in line. Or when Joanna is fussy, I take her on my lap in the rocking chair and begin to hum, letting my mind drift up to you with a simple "Thank you, God."

Pray for yourself, pray for others, try a prayer break today!

A Matter of Trust

Many will see and fear, and put their trust in the Lord (Ps. 40:3).

My neighbor had her baby yesterday in the same hospital where Joanna was born, and I dropped in to see them both. I must confess I was a bit shocked at this tiny, red, wrinkled new arrival. I don't remember Joanna looking so withered on her first day. To me she was the most exquisitely beautiful creature in the entire world. But later my husband confirmed that Joanna, indeed, was born red and wrinkled. Such is the myopic vision of mother, I had already forgotten.

I haven't forgotten, though, how kind and helpful were the superb nurses in the labor and delivery rooms. They were reassuring, stayed close to me, and were genuinely compassionate. I trusted them completely.

O Lord, how important it is to trust. I trust the grocer to provide me with produce that is fresh and good, the credit card company trusts me to pay the bill I owe, I trust the doctor's diagnosis for Joanna. The whole fabric of the world is woven of trust. At its core is the trust that family members build with each other. Strengthened by such trust, they can move confidently in their sphere. This, in turn, is based on our trust in you, Lord. When we express trust in you with all our words and deeds, we express the highest truth we know. Help me to teach Joanna this kind of trust.

That Was Wonderful, Mom!

That the love with which thou has loved me may be in them, and I in them (John 17:26).

I rested on a bench in the shopping mall the other afternoon and heard a child's voice on the other side cut through the din around me. "That was wonderful, Mom!" The voice was so full of pleasure and praise and pride that I wondered what on earth Mom had done or said to cause such a response. Most of us expect love to grow naturally, but it has to be nurtured.

A friend confided to me that she grew up in a home without love. Her parents, she said, cared for her physical wants, but seemed unable to express their love or else just could not feel it. "I was a teenager before I discovered this. I had to learn to love on my own, and it hasn't been simple. I'm still learning," she concluded sadly.

We shouldn't ever take love for granted. How fortunate is the family where love flows deep and supportive. It can make the difference between living successfully and being defeated.

Lord, be present in the hearts of my husband and me and Joanna. Lead us to love her with your reflecting love, so that she may grow into a loving, caring child. Let me hear her say sometimes, "That was wonderful, Mom!"

A Mother's Song

And Mary said, "My soul magnifies the Lord, and my spirit rejoices in God my Savior" (Luke 1:46).

Send up the balloons, bring on the band, set off the fireworks. Today we are celebrating Joanna's first birthday!

What an incredible year this has been. I, who am overflowing with imagination, could not have envisioned the richness and dimension this child has brought into our lives. Such a beautiful baby, Joanna, full of happiness, affection, and yes, intelligence. To follow a baby's progress from a completely helpless infant to a young child poised on the edge of independent action and thought is a remarkable privilege. Forgotten are the sleepless nights, the mountains of laundry, the food messes. We may have other children, but the thrill of first parenthood will remain in my memory as an awesome, inspiring journey. What lasting gifts can I bring our child in celebration?

Lord, let me give her love, and thought, and joy, and the certainty that her family circle is strong. Hold me back when I am tempted to interfere and not let her make her own mistakes. Above all, God, lead me as I teach her about you. Bless the loving efforts of my husband and me as we try to draw out the gifts of kindness, compassion, and service to others you have placed in her heart. Enhance all our lives with your divine presence, and smile with us as we sing, "Happy Birthday, Joanna!"